"STILL ON THE RISE TO *Achieving* GREATNESS"

**BY
LAUREN C. WARD**

Copyright © 2016, Lauren C. Ward
Still On the Rise to Achieving Greatness

ISBN 13: 978-1-939654-77-9
IBSN 10: 1-939654-77-7

All rights reserved solely by the author. Except where designated, the author certifies that all contents are original and do not infringe upon the legal rights of any other person or work. No part of this book may be reproduced in any form without the permission of the publisher.

Printed in the United States
10 9 8 7 6 5 4 3 2 1

Cover design by: Tasha Sykes
                    Legacy Designs, Inc.
                    Legacydesigninc@gmail.com

Published by:
Life To Legacy, LLC
2441 Vermont Street, #57
Blue Island, IL 60406
(877) 267-7477
www.Life2Legacy.com

Presented to:

Contact the author at:
Lward98@gmail.com

Contents

Dedication — 5

Acknowledgments — 6

1. The Journey Continues — 8
2. Building Your Empire — 20
3. Closer Than You Think — 43
4. When Life Happens — 54
5. Accepting Where You Are — 62
6. Giving Yourself Credit — 66

Dedication

This book is dedicated to my astonishing and beautiful parents, Marilyn and Yogi Ward. They are an irreplaceable canvas that will always rank number one in my life.

I also dedicate this book to my students and my mentees. The bond I share with them is beyond special. Words cannot express how special they are to me.

Acknowledgments

First and foremost, I thank my parents, Marilyn and Yogi Ward, for giving me the support, guidance, and motivation I needed to write my first book. They have been by my side since the beginning and they will always be my guardian angels. I thank my grandma, Johnnie Mae Greer, for being the example of what black excellence truly represents and for being the matriarch in my family. I want to thank my aunties Marsha Greer, Lauren Greer, Lynn Napoleon and Mary Farrell. I also want to thank my uncles John Ward and Victor Ward.

I especially want to thank my cousins who feel more like siblings. My older sister, Ashley Shambley, younger sister, Brittany Jett and little brother Brandon Redmond for loving me endlessly and being the rocks in my life I can always count on. I would also like to thank my other cousins who have been supportive of my dreams. Tiffany, Rasheed, Bernadette, Natasha, Jalen, Karolina, Maryah, Ravan, Reall, Marshona, Skye, Skylar, Sukena, Chandler and Jen Jen. I would like to thank my grandparents, Victor Ward and Mary Ward, for their continuous love and support.

I want to thank my devoted and loving boyfriend of six

years, Tyshaun "Ty" Martin for always being my best friend, my better half and my clear skies after a storm.

I want to thank my mentors, Dr. Anthony Gantt, Carolyn Arthur, Karen Coleman, Edward Hancock, Andrew Wells, Jason Johnson, Sandra Robinson, Cheryl Burton, Evelyn Holmes, Dr. Winston Johnson, and Rev. Derrick B Wells because whenever I need advice or prayer I can always call on these individuals.

I also want to thank Dr. Dennis and Chantia Woods for their continued support because they helped me get my first book published and now they have helped me to get my second book off the ground. I'm extremely grateful to have them in my corner and I thank God for placing a power couple in my circle, because what this couple has done for me will never be forgotten.

My deepest appreciation to other family members, friends, sorority sisters, extended family and fans who have given me their wisdom, support and unconditional love. All of you have inspired me to write this book and I will continue to follow my dreams.

Chapter One
The Journey Continues

Welcome Back to Lwoo Landddddd!!!!!!

Today's words of the day are "I'm Back." I have learned a lot since 2014 and one thing I cherish most from that year is my book because it was the start to new beginnings. My first book, opened doors for me I thought were impossible to walk through. My book inspired people to have a relationship with God.

It helped people continue on with school, it made people go back to school, it helped to elevate people's careers, motivated people to move out of their parent's house, (myself included), given strength to those who needed to repair their relationships with their significant others, empowered many to realize their worth and it has encouraged a lot of people to look toward having a family of their own one day.

I prayed to God that I would change lives and I have. I asked God to reveal my purpose because I told God I want to use my voice to walk in my truth. I told Him I want to lead people closer to Him and closer to their dreams. I receive fulfillment from helping others because I have blessed them with love, knowledge and service. God is so good because in the process of me helping others he blessed me. I didn't think I had enough courage to step out on faith and follow my dreams but I challenged myself and as a result, I'm thankful that I did because I inspired others to do the same.

My journey is not done but to see that it is continuing on is a blessing. The progress that I have made from last year into this year gives me chills because I never thought I would experience joy, peace and security any time soon. I was unemployed, living at home with my parents and trying to make ends meet off of a savings account that was slowly but surely fading away. The last sentence in my first book is one of my favorite quotes that I have written:

"Pay attention to the signs in life because when you feel like giving up that's when your next blessing will present itself."

This quote, always has allowed me to push through because whenever I feel defeated God always sends an angel my way to remind me of my gift. Whether that's receiving a positive comment on social media or someone just reminding me of the role I play in their life, God is always on time!

After everything I've been through, I understand what it means to be the chosen one because God picked me to be his faithful servant to influence a nation. There is a reason why I couldn't find a job, there is a reason why after college I needed to move back in with my parents, there is a reason why I had thoughts of suicide, there is a reason why all my jobs are temporary, there is a reason why he gave me a good man, and there is a reason why he made sure I had both of my parents in my life. He strategically set my life up this way because He knew if there were no test there would be no testimony. Even though I experienced a lot of pain in feeling less than by working a minimum wage job, especially when I have two degrees, I know God never gave me more than I can handle. He prepared me for my next steps because he knew I was going to need those lessons so I could stay above water.

The Bible says, "To whom much is given, much is required," and I needed God to prepare me and remind me of this. If I ever have a moment where I begin to sink I will know what to do so I won't drown. Preparation is what He gave me and trust is what I gained from God. I learned that when you let go and let God you really have to do that because if you are still worried about the problem that means you don't trust the Lord to handle it. So now when I let go and let God, I don't worry anymore about what I was stressing over because I know God will handle it better than I can.

Many are called but only few are chosen and you have to ask yourself if you are the chosen one? Sometimes God will test you just to see if you trust Him and to pass the challenge the first thing you have to do is believe in Him.

Here, I am saying I want a fulltime job with salary and benefits but that's not my calling. He purposely won't give me that because when he gave it to me in 2011 I almost passed on graduate school for it, so this time around he wants me to give all of my energy to LWOO. LWOO stands for Lauren Ward Overcoming Obstacles and it also stands for Learning Wisdom Optimism and Opportunity. The first acronym represents my for profit, which is LWOO Enterprises. The second acronym represents my non-for-profit, LWOO, NFP. With these two organizations I plan to give back in my community by empowering young people and adults to become entrepreneurs. God is disciplining me to stay on task because he needs me to complete my journey. I have different states, countries, homes, churches and shelters to travel to so he can't allow me to become distracted. He knows that if I get tied down to a job I won't be able to deliver his will to his people. I have come too far and there is no job that can define my worth. How is it that you spend 40 hours a week on a job but it's still not enough? Working paycheck to pay check and your barely making ends meet?

I don't want that lifestyle and I don't want that lifestyle for you either. Don't get me wrong, a job is a good thing to have in order for you to pay your bills, build your savings account and feed yourself but what's your plan to truly step into your God given purpose? Are you supposed to be working that job for the rest of your life or are you suppose to have your own business? That's just something I want you to think about.

I currently work three jobs but as I stated earlier, they're all temporary because God needs me to stay focused on LWOO. One of the jobs is for nine months and the other two are for seven months. I don't mind assisting with the other two programs because they are after school but the reality is all three of the jobs are temporary. At first, I was a little worried about the fact that they weren't permanent but it actually worked in my favor because it has given me more time to focus on my career which is getting LWOO off the ground. Every time I get a paycheck I take the money to pay my bills, buy groceries, put some in my savings account and most of all, spend it on building LWOO. If you have to work a job make sure you are putting some money aside for your business, travel, home purchase or a car purchase. Think about your future and don't be comfortable with where you are. Push yourself to want the BEST and not just enough to get by. I believe that we weren't put on this earth to struggle. We were put here to live a prosperous, happy and successful life. I believe that we were put here to help one another strive for excellence and I know in my heart that we are suppose to help every individual obtain that. No man or woman should be left behind.

Hey Readers, let me get even more personal with you. Did you know that God specifically designed a vision for you and for me before we were even born? Did you know that he has already prepared your purpose and he already knew what you were supposed to be doing? I know some of you may be answering "YES!" too these questions so I'm telling you right now don't waste any more time. You already had that idea and that thought when you woke up this morning. God wouldn't have placed it in your heart if he felt like you couldn't achieve it. He put that dream in your heart for a reason so I'm here to tell you it wasn't a mistake. Dream big and dream wide and understand that your imagination is bigger than what you see in front of you. It might be invisible but God will make it visible. Don't become complacent with mediocrity because you have to remember that you are God's masterpiece. You are the living creation that he is using to empower others. You are his number one soldier and he needs you to lead the pack. It only takes one person to make a difference and you my friend are the one he's been waiting on to break free.

He's waiting on you to tap into your gift. So, use your gift and stop sitting on your talent. Begin to create multiple streams of income because God made you multi-faceted for a reason. You may be pursuing a career in the medical field but that hasn't stopped you from having thoughts about doing hair. You may be working in the education field but that hasn't stopped you from having thoughts about owning your own business. You can do it all.

This could be your time to fulfill your purpose. You have to walk in it, claim it, own it, and execute it like there is no tomorrow. Work that job for now and save your money but have a plan of how you can start your own business in the future. Build a legacy that can benefit not only you but also your children and their children's children.

You have all the ingredients within you to be successful. You have to be proud about who you are. You have to be proud about how far you've come. Give yourself credit for graduating high school, college or maybe even law school. Give yourself credit for getting a promotion on your job or quitting your job to start your own company. At the end of the day, I just want you to be happy and I don't want you to put any limitations on yourself. I think everyone deserves to live a lifestyle of abundance and stability but if your current job or situation isn't providing that then what's wrong with creating your own opportunity? It's you that has to write the ending to your story so if you don't like what you see then rewrite the script. God has a plan for your life that no man can take away and if you become the pilot of your plane you wont look for validation from the co-pilot because you know you got this.

I stated that the journey continues on because my work isn't done until I inspire the world. I have taken the time to invest in myself and I want the world to know that if they take a little extra time to write that book, finish that painting, start that fashion line, build that consulting firm or audition for that play you can inspire people and change the world, too. The best investment is investing in yourself because it is the most authentic thing you can give to the world and to yourself. To be honest, you owe it to yourself to figure out how unique and talented you are.

You may be so dope that they don't even have your talent in stock anymore. To be honest, the cloth you were cut from is so rare it doesn't exist anymore.

You have to remember that you can't be duplicated because you're an original so more than likely the shelf will be empty when people go searching for your God given talent. So begin to value your talent and the person you are. No one will ever value you as much as you value yourself. I'm encouraging you to step outside of your comfort zone and create opportunities that will be endless for you and your family. It's no fun to struggle and why should anyone have to? I don't know about everyone else but I like having options. If I want to travel, buy a yacht, a BMW or even a summer home in another state I want to be able to do that and not only purchase it but enjoy it. Some people work so hard that they don't even get to see the fruits of their labor and that's no fun either.

My advice to you is to call or email a local college in your area, inquire about their small business development center, make an appointment and go in with your business plan. Entrepreneurship is beginning to take over the world because Corporate America and other career fields are dying off. Instead of being caught in the pool of unemployment like I was for several years, think ahead of the game. For years I was trying to figure out why employers continuously told me I was overqualified or that I needed more experience. I had to accept that my talent was too big for their company. I said, "Lauren, you are such an amazing person that you don't fit in with working for companies because God has something much bigger in store for you."

The same way they're saying "You Can't Sit With Us," well guess what, when you become successful they're going to be begging you to sit at their table. The conversation may go a little something like this.

"Excuse me is this LWOO's table? Why yes it is!"

"Oh ok I'm not on the list but she knows me and we go wayyyyy back." "Righttttt. Aren't you the employer that said she was overqualified?"

"Uuuuum yeah but…" "Girl Bye! Hahahahaha it's too late to jump on the bandwagon now. Where were you when she needed a job?"

So young people have enough faith to start your own company. You don't deserve to have an employer say if you're qualified or not. You already know you are because you are a child of God so when you get rejected take that as a sign that you were too GREAT for that position. You were too BIG for that company and recognize that you are LARGER than life. Will people talk about you? Yes, they will. Will people think that your confidence has turned into cockiness? Yes they will. But they don't understand how God has taken a blurry vision and made it clear JUST FOR YOU! They don't understand how God has allowed you to see your worth so that you can tap into your fullest potential. God will become your biggest cheerleader because he knows what it feels like to have haters. Jesus Christ experienced betrayal, bullying and abuse but if he rose up on the third day despite everything he had been through then he is telling you that you can do it too. So understand that they missed out on an opportunity to experience you, not the other way around. Keep smiling, keep being positive, keep praying and keep working hard because the journey continues on but it will only continue if you don't give up.

By 30, my plan is to have LWOO Enterprises and LWOO NFP in several schools, churches, shelters and youth centers across the world. I will be traveling as a well-known motivational speaker, author, actress, talk show host and entrepreneur. I plan on being the next best thing because My God said I CAN! Some people don't believe me when I say I'm going to be as big as Oprah or T.D. Jakes but I don't mind because the God I serve said I CAN! He is the game changer. He is the alpha and the omega, he is the way shower, he can make crooked places straight and he can make no way out of any way. My 6 Step Plan has become a reality because of God and now I'm halfway there to achieving my GREATNESS. If God said I CAN then how can a human say I can't. I understand my purpose! Now that God has given me my assignment, I must go forth and share it with the world. I have his approval and that is all I need to shine bright like a diamond.

Grab your pen and paper now because before we go on to the next chapter I want you to answer these questions!!
- If you could start your own business, what would it be?
- Do you know how to create a business plan?
- Do you know how to market your business properly?
- Do you feel you have enough knowledge to successfully run a business?
- If you get fired or laid off from your job tomorrow, what do you have to fall back on?

Chapter 2
Building My Empire

Welcomeeeeeee to LWOOOOOO LANDDDDDDDDDDDDDDDDDDDDDDDDDD AGAINNNNNNN!!!!!!! Well ladies and gentlemen, I'm proud to say that I'm building my empire and it's coming along well. Since the last time I wrote to you I have been in three movies, two plays, signed to a talent agency, two managers, connected with one of my favorite motivational speakers, incorporated my non profit for girls and boys, wrote my first and second book, a talk-show on YouTube called the LWOO show, and I started inspirational posts on social media everyday. You may be familiar with my Motivational Monday, Tenacious Tuesday, Winning Wednesday, Thankful Thursday and Freestyle Friday.

You may even be familiar with my theme song on my website at www.lwoo.org but wherever you've been getting your daily dosage of LWOO, I'm grateful you've become one of my supporters.

In 2015, I traveled to Jamaica, DC, Georgia, and Colorado for my birthday ski trip. I also worked at the Chicago Urban League over the summer as a youth mentor and they recently hired me back on for another temporary assignment. In this particular role, I had the opportunity to go to New York for a week for an all expense paid trip to receive training on how to teach the Black Community about healthy eating and healthy living. I had never gone on an all-expense-paid trip for a job so I was extremely appreciative for the opportunity. Not only did they pay for our flights and hotel room but they gave us spending money too. I was in heaven.

This experience made me realize God had been working tirelessly to take me to the next level. To take you back to 2014, I want to briefly remind you about my book signing. It was extremely successful and the book signing left me on cloud 9. I sold out of all of my books, t-shirts and cd's. I premiered my newest music video at my book release party and I performed one of my motivational raps. It was a magical night and I'll never forget it!!

Two months later, I quickly realized that I couldn't just relax on one book, my t-shirts and cd's. I was thinking that my product could catapult me into my destiny but I had to keep working because my journey to success and God's kingdom was just beginning. I'm not going to lie, that was a hard pill to swallow because my mind was saying "Haven't I done enough already," but my spirit said, "Your journey has just begun."

BUCKLE UP FOLKS BECAUSE HERE'S HOW THE EMPIRE BEGAN

Winter of 2015, I started working at Macy's because I told myself I needed the income in order to keep buying more books from my publisher so that I could sell them to my customers. I had no idea that $100 would only get me 16 books. Although I'm extremely grateful that my publisher's published my book for free that doesn't take away the fact that I still have to purchase my product like several other authors so I can sell it to my customers. The procedure for my books to be sent to me can be costly. The books are always high quality when I receive them but when you're trying to save money along with building an empire you have to figure out ways to stay in business and also keep money in your pocket. Now I understand why people say it's important to invest in yourself because you have to be willing to spend some money but also know how important it is to budget your money as well. But what if you don't have the money to get started? What if every time you get paid, your money goes to your bills? Here's the catch. Are you a great saver? If you're not, then challenge yourself to save more money and make more sacrifices for your future. Young people, I'm thankful for my savings account and I happen to be a great saver. I've been able to get by with purchasing more books due to my savings account. So if that means holding off on buying new clothes, new shoes, video games or music then I'll do it. Just to be truthful though, sometimes you begin to dig in your savings account when you have no income coming in and of course that can become a major problem. I get it. I've been there. That's actually when I realized that in order for me to purchase more books, keep my savings account at a decent amount and pay my bills, I was going to need a consistent paycheck.

Whelp, it was a hard decision but I went back to retail. As I stated earlier, I started back working at Macy's. I loved the people I worked with but gosh darn it, I couldn't stand the store manager and some of the customers were out right rude. My co-workers and I would laugh about the unfriendly customers and about the store manager but after a while, I got fed up with all of it. Especially because when I took the job I told them I could only work a certain time on the weekends. I explained to them that my Monday through Friday would be open and they agreed to that but shortly after I started, that agreement became void. They scheduled me to work weekends. They had me closing down the store and working over 8 hours sometimes. I said to myself

"Wait a minute, this wasn't the plan. I was part-time and

it began to feel like I was full-time."

Hellooooo!!!!! Don't you know I have speaking engagements, book signings and movies to perform in? I was so adamant to let people know that I wouldn't be at this retail store for long that I started bringing my books to work and selling it. Hahahahahahaha!!!! I started to sell my product and I was passing out my business cards at the same time. I took down associate's contact information and I promoted my own business. I told myself if I was going to be working late nights and weekends here I might as well get something out of it that would help launch my business. But then I received my first paycheck and Oh Lord, it wasn't what I expected. I said to myself after all these hours I worked I only made $230??? Are you kidding me????? That's not enough money for my phone bill, credit card, car insurance, gas or other bills I needed to pay. They were working me like a Hebrew slave but I wasn't seeing any growth so I decided to walk away from that opportunity. I started doing more speaking engagements, selling my books and acting. I created my own talk show and started doing my inspirational posts on social media. Although the money wasn't consistent with my books and speaking engagements, it made me happy. It allowed me to see my vision turn into a reality. A month later, I was so worried about leaving that retail store and I began to second-guess my decision but then I went to church and the Pastor said "Just trust in the Lord." As soon as I let go and let God he blessed me with a job opportunity at the Chicago Urban League as a Youth Mentor. I was able to talk about my book, motivate my students to have self-respect, I taught them about gardening, and how to build a bike. I said

"God what did I do to land this perfect job opportunity?" The pay was way more, too. I earned $1,500 or more every two weeks, which was a blessing. Unfortunately, it was only for the summer but I was extremely grateful that I was selected to be apart of the Green Corp Program. The Green Corp Program was an opportunity that taught me and the youth how to build bikes from scratch, it taught us that all bikes are designed differently, how to grow flowers, how to properly take care of gardens and it gave the adults an opportunity to motivate the youth about career goals and college because we were with them on a day to day basis.

Great things were happening to me left and right and the next thing that happened to me was that I got signed with a Talent Agency. Now, let me explain something, I had been trying to get with this agency since the Winter of 2014. I was referred to them by my mentor, who is close to one of the women that run the agency but that wasn't enough to get me signed. I was told that they didn't know how to cast me since I juggled so many different hats. After the agency told me no in 2014 l went crazy because Lauren C. Ward A.K.A. LWOO doesn't take no for an answer. I was determined to help them see how talented I was so I went into over drive with trying to build my brand.

I did a music video called "Lauren Ward End The Violence Feat. Saint The Good Boy." I was an extra on "Empire", I was a stand in on Empire for a famous singer and I did some extra work on "Chicago Fire." As young people say I was "on my grind," because I didn't want them to deny me again. I didn't want to solely depend on this talent agency either, so I sent my stuff out to several talent agencies and I ended up getting connected with a woman who was signed with a major talent agency in Chicago. She was able to get me an audition at this talent agency and I nailed the audition. However, I wasn't selected because the agency was at full capacity when I applied. The agency is small so they want to make sure they don't take on to many clients because they want to get their current talent work. I was hurt but I understood. One of my friends from Howard University is signed with them so when she broke it down to me it made sense and she told me don't give up just reapply again. By the way, Howard University is where I graduated from in 2011 with my B.A. in Broadcast Journalism and a minor in acting. I also graduated from Northwestern University in 2012 with my M.S. in Communications. I just wanted to clarify that in case you didn't read my first book but moving right along.

I was waiting for six months to pass by so I could reapply again and in the mean time I auditioned for a film called, "The Breath Of Winslow Belle." I was thrilled when I got the part to play Pearl. You know how the famous Wayan's family has their whole family involved in film that's how the Bass family is. Their whole family is involved in film and I think it's so cool. It was an honor to work with them and I hope to work with them again in the future. The film will be out in film festivals and possibly even theaters in 2016. I was super excited about that too because I couldn't wait to invite my family and close friends to see the first viewing of the movie. I felt like a celebrity. I was beginning to get happy again because I'm like wow I did all of this work on my own without an agent, so I knew when I reached out again there would be no way they could deny me. I reached out again and they said they would get back to me but I felt that I had waited long enough. I texted one of the agents and I asked her if I could just come in and audition for her. I was in shock when she texted me back and said yes. The day of my audition I was driving to the destination and right when I got outside of the building she said that the casting crew had to reschedule. I told her I was downstairs already and she said I'm so sorry but you'll have to come back again. I was really sad and angry because I knew in my heart if they just gave me five minutes I could knock their socks off.

I began to cry in my car because I didn't know what to do and at that point I began to feel defeated. God made me dry up my tears quickly though because the talent agency called back and told me to come on up. I said you have to be kidding me. Boyyyyy I dried up those tears, put back on my shoes, and strutted up to the third floor. The agents told me they changed their minds once they realized I was really downstairs. I did my monologue and I did a cold read for them. They asked me to step outside of the door and they would call me back in after they make a decision. I sat there quietly but I was praying constantly. I kept saying to myself God if this is for me then who can be against me. I kept saying this is mine and it has my name written all over it so I'm taking it.

"Lauren, can you come back in please. We have made a decision?" I walked back in and I thought my heart was going to fall out of my body. I was sweating bullets too. They said, "It was a tough decision but we would like to officially welcome you to our agency!!!" I said

"HOT DIGGETY DOG I DID IT YEAAAAAAA BOYYYYY." I was so geeked I called all of my family, my boyfriend, Ty and my close friends. I felt like I had accomplished one of my goals and now I could check that off the list. I couldn't stop smiling, crying and leaping for joy.

I told my friend who was signed at another agency about it and she was beyond excited but she reminded me that the work doesn't stop there. It's nice to have an agent but just because you get signed that doesn't mean you should stop booking your own gigs. So I didn't stop looking. I ended up getting cast in a play called "Preachin & Creepin." The director didn't even have a part for me but she was so intrigued with my talent that she wrote a part for me. I felt extremely blessed and I couldn't stop thanking her for including me in her play that she had already casted. During the play, I was still working at the Chicago Urban League but I had no idea God wasn't done with me yet.

Do you know that I got another phone call from my agent saying that Tika Sumpter from the hit show, "The Haves and The Have Nots" needed a stand-in? It turns out that they were shooting a movie in Chicago called "South Side With You." The agency told me that it was a movie about Barack Obama and Michelle Robinson. I was still trying to wrap my mind around the part of being in the same room as Tika Sumpter, I couldn't believe I was being picked to work on a movie about The President of The United States and the First Lady. I thought to myself is my agent really calling me to be apart of this project? I was speechless.

I told my agent without hesitation that I would take the job. There was one problem though; I was still working a full time job. I thank God for the boss I had because if anyone believed in my dreams, Mr. Hancock always did. He was extremely supportive and he understood why I had to leave. I'm also thankful to have Mr. Wells, Mr. Parker, and Ms. Karen Coleman in my life because those are three people at the Urban League who assisted me with trying to find employment. Those were three people who weren't going to allow me to give up. Mr. Hancock and his staff believed in my dreams and I couldn't have asked for a better group of people to be connected with. They were extremely supportive so I left the Urban League in July of 2015 and I went full speed ahead with the movie project. It was definitely a major pay cut but I didn't care because I was doing something I loved.

Overall, it was a great experience because Tika Sumpter was genuine, helpful and really sweet. I gave her and Parker Sawyers who will be playing Barack Obama a complimentary copy of my book. Parker Sawyers was extremely helpful and nice as well. It was really cool to see how much he and Obama looked alike. The best part is I got both of their contact information and they both keep in contact with me. They have given me great advice and I hope to work with them again very soon. I would say the hardest part about the project was saying goodbye because I really did get to work with some amazing people. Oh and did I forget to mention that the food was always on point!!!! That's one thing I can say about show business they feed you well.

If I had to choose another hard part to get accustomed to it would probably be working the long hours because sometimes you're on set for 12 to 16 hours. This experience also taught me how to be patient along with accepting constructive criticism because you get yelled at a lot. Man people weren't lying when they said show business isn't all glitz and glam because it definitely wasn't. There were some days when it was extremely hot outside but we were still filming. There were some days when it was extremely cold outside but we were still filming. As I stated previously, there were some days where we would start work at 6p.m. and we wouldn't finish until 6 or 7a.m.

The experience was definitely worth it but I know what I'm getting myself into now, which is what I needed. Last but not least, I have to mention my co-star, Lee Albritton, who was absolutely amazing. He was down to earth, gave great advice and had a beautiful spirit. When I found out he was Bernie Mac's manager for 13 years I was overly excited. Everyone knows that I love imitating Bernie Mac and he was definitely one of my role models. Lee told me about how Bernie Mac was growing up and he shared with me Bernie's journey to success, which I was very appreciative of. Lee's testimony about his own trials and tribulations along with Bernie's testimony really inspired me to keep going. So despite all the chaos that sometimes happened on set, Lee and I didn't allow that to affect our experience. We left on a good note and we were happy that our talent agency blessed us with that opportunity.

After the production was finished, I left town to travel to Jamaica for my 5 Year Anniversary with my line sisters. This vacation changed my perspective about life and it motivated me to take a vacation like this every year. It was perfect. I just wrapped up on my movie and then I headed out for my international trip to Jamaica Mon what more could I ask for? Jamaica was the bomb and that's definitely somewhere I want to visit again. We stayed in Ocho Rios and the resort was beautiful. It was all-inclusive which is something I never experienced before, so my line sisters and I kind of went crazy at the resort. The ocean was clear and the weather was perfect. We went swimming with the dolphins; we did community service by donating over a 100 books to young girls to teach them about loving themselves and having self-worth. We also wrote them a check for $5,000 so that was an amazing feeling. I was extremely excited because I was able to donate a few of my books too, which was truly a blessing. After we did the community service we climbed a waterfall, we had our own personal yacht, we had a sisterly relations night, we went to clubs, we went shopping and so much more. It was one of the best vacations I've ever had. I even had the opportunity to go up on the stage and announce to the world who LWOO was.

My line sisters weren't expecting for me to get past security but as soon as they turned their head I was up on stage dancing, talking about Chicago and singing my theme song about LWOO. My line sisters were cracking up and the security started to come get me off the stage but then they were like forget it she's from America let her have some fun. I also crashed a wedding OH MY GOODNESS that was fun. I've never done that before. Thank God the bride was ok with it to or else that could've gone badly but my line sisters were with me so we started partying with the bride. Awwww man I can definitely say great memories were created on that trip because of all the crazy nights we had.

Did you know that from this experience several of my line sisters bought my book in Jamaica to the point where I was overwhelmed with tears? Even a woman I didn't know named Ms. Sandra bought my book. I met her in Chicago at the airport and it turned out that we were staying at the same resort. What were the odds of that? On the day I left the resort she found me in the lobby and bought my book. I was a little worried on the plane ride to Jamaica. I kept thinking my movie project is finished and I won't have anything to return home to because I'll be unemployed, but God said no need to worry. I'll bring you revenue from your books and I was beyond grateful. When I returned I had money from the books I sold, I had some speaking engagements booked, I kept doing my inspirational posts, I kept enhancing my talk show, I followed up with my agents and I began to seek management. There was only one problem. Although I made some good money in Jamaica from my books, I still needed more. I told myself I need a consistent income in order to pay my bills, build up my savings account and move out of my parent's house. I said to myself, "It's a blessing for me to have two parents that provide for me, cook for me and love me but how long am I going to depend on them?"

I want my own source of income and my own place so

I can start taking care of them by sending them on trips, giving back to my community and just being independent. Even though my parents never said to me I have to take care of them I think as an only child I just feel obligated to. I wouldn't be the woman I am today without them so that's why I'm determined to give back.

I hate to say it but I began to look for a job again and I felt bad because I knew I was suppose to keep building my empire but I explained to God that I needed more money to do that. The only thing is I wasn't getting hired. I applied for a full-time job and it was looking extremely well with me landing the job but in the last interview the employer appeared intimidated by me. She saw I had my master's degree so she knew they would have to pay me more and the next thing I knew I received a phone call saying that they decided to move forward with another candidate. When I didn't get the job I was disappointed because a similar situation had happened earlier in the year. I couldn't understand why the women at these companies would be threatened by me because I didn't want their job. I just wanted a job. I was angry and I knew it was only a matter of time before I heard from God and I did.

He said LWOO what are you doing? Why do you keep looking for a job when I helped you create your books, I helped you build your talk show and I gave you the idea for your inspirational posts? I just want you to keep the faith so after he reminded me of that I did exactly what he wanted. I stopped looking for a job and I got my license to become a street peddler downtown. Now, I sell my books, t-shirts and do my motivational speaking downtown. I have a bookstand that I created and I use my radio to play my theme song, my motivational raps and my motivational speeches. I have earned a consistent income from doing this.

I finally figured out what God had done. He said if you do something for me I'll do something for you, so after I started selling my product downtown as a street peddler, focusing on my talk show and doing the inspirational posts everyday, faithfully, he knew I was listening to him and that I was being obedient. Which is why he blessed me with the Urban League job opportunity as a Healthy Living Peer Educator. God knew with a full-time job I wouldn't be able to finish my business plan, my second book, hustle downtown and get my building for my non-profit. He also knew I wouldn't be able to fly back and forth to LA for auditions. He knew I had much bigger plans and he couldn't allow anything or anyone to distract me. God also blessed me with an opportunity to work at another organization, which was another temporary job opportunity but I wasn't able to take it. It conflicted with the Urban League but the fact that I had options was something I was grateful for. Although the Chicago Urban League was a temporary position, it was perfect for me because it gave me time to still build my empire. It was easier to build my empire now because I had the money to do so. I was working at the Chicago Urban League, getting my not-for-profit off the ground and working downtown as a street peddler/street performer. Shoot, I even told myself I could pick up another part-time job and start driving Uber if I wanted to but the point is God made a way out of no way. He turned my passion into a career, so that I could start earning income. He blessed me with some temporary jobs just to give me a consistent income in case there are some days when my business is slow. I also realized that God put me at the Urban League because there was a potential possibility that they could partner with LWOO Enterprises or LWOO NFP and become a permanent sponsor. It never crossed my mind about partnering with a prestigious organization but when God put the seed in my head I realized that the Chicago Urban League has been around for 100 years. They have helped African Americans and people in general get jobs, create businesses and get funding for it. The Urban League could be a potential client for my business and that is a huge deal because of the respect, popularity and trust they have established in several communities.

Here I was, complaining that things weren't working out after I got back from Jamaica and God was paving a way for me the whole time. He told me to just be patient and appreciate the days I'm at home because I can work on building my empire. Once I figured out the secret from God I was at home building my brand during the months of September and October.

I prayed on getting managers and God blessed me with them. I told God I wanted to finish my second book and he made that possible. He helped me to revise my business plan, he helped me to start getting space for my non-profit, he helped me to get my non profit incorporated, he helped me to get casted for another play and for two movies. The second film I did was so cool because I was able to do it with my boyfriend, Ty. Ty isn't an actor. He's more behind the scenes but the point is he stepped out of his comfort zone to be in front of the camera and that meant the world to me. It's called "The Crazy Household," and it's about a husband and a wife having martial problems, but in the end they work it all out.

To take it back, after Jamaica I wanted to keep traveling and God made that possible. God allowed me to go to St.

Louis for a family vacation, I went to the Classics in Chicago with my family, and I traveled to DC for part two of my five-year anniversary with my line sisters. I went to my line sisters wedding in Atlanta, I went to my line sister's wedding in New Orleans and Colorado for my birthday ski trip. God really showed me that if I just trust in his plan he will make sure I'm rewarded. He reminded me that my work is different from other people. It might not be the traditional work that corporate America does but it's work because I'm working hard everyday to make my legacy GREAT!!! Whether I'm downtown selling books, at home writing another book, doing teen writing workshops, shooting a music video, or working at the Urban League it's all hard work. After what God has shown me, who am I to question his plan for my life? All those times I thought about giving up he reassured me that everything would be ok. How dare I go out there and look for a full-time job after God told me what I needed to do to be successful. How dare I try to give up on my dream when I gave a speech in 2011 about never giving up on your dreams!

This is what I said in one of my most popular speeches on YouTube:

"How dare you want to give up on your dreams when in, 1850 Harriet Tubman freed slaves for you, how dare you

want to give up on your dreams when in,

1964 Nelson Mandela spent 27 years in prison for you, how dare you want to give up on your dreams when in,

1968 Dr. Martin Luther King was assassinated for you, how dare you want to give up on your dreams when in,

2009 Barack Obama became the first African American president for you, how dare you want to give up on your dreams when on the third day Jesus Christ rose just for you. How dare you? How dare you? I had a dream that I would graduate from Howard University and obtain my bachelors, I had a dream that I would graduate from Northwestern University and obtain my masters, I had a dream that I would become apart of Phi Sigma Pi National Honor Fraternity and I had a dream that I would become apart of Alpha Kappa Alpha Sorority, Incorporated, Alpha Chapter and I achieved that. And if you think my God is done with me then you just don't know my God because he's just getting started."

This is one of my favorite quotes that I said in my speech at Christ Universal Temple and sometimes I have to motivate myself from my own words so I won't give up. I have to keep building my empire because my family, my close friends, my boyfriend and my unborn children are counting on me to WIN!!!!!!!

It takes discipline, commitment, confidence and faith to create something from scratch. In your heart you know it's going to be successful but in your mind you might be a little nervous. This is your time to shine so be fearless when you are building your empire. Don't worry about failing because it's the failures that people want to hear about so they can learn how to overcome obstacles they're dealing with. Don't give up on building your empire because I promise you someone is rooting for you to win, someone is watching your success everyday and they are inspired by it.

You don't know who you are breathing life into and if you stop writing those inspirational posts, if you stop building your empire, if you stop blogging about your experience of embracing your natural hair, if you stop coaching that basketball team, if you stop sharing your journey with God, if you stop opening up about your struggles then someone will stop living life and they will only exist in it. If you quit then someone watching you will lose hope, feel emptiness and be saddened. Let's not give the enemy the satisfaction of seeing that happen so keep fighting to fulfill your dreams and don't allow anyone or anything to steal what God put your name on a long time ago. Remember the enemy comes to steal, kill and destroy so fight against the enemy because your joy, your experiences and your knowledge is needed to save our nation.

Grab your pen and paper again! Let's Go!

- Do you want to build an empire?
- What legacy do you want to leave behind with this empire?
- Are you afraid that it won't be successful? If so, why?
- Do you know who to contact to help build your empire?
- Why do you think building an empire is important?

Chapter 3
Closer Than You Think

In 2015, I realized that I am closer than I think I am to achieving every dream, every vision and goal I set for myself. I have been scared, confused and worried because I felt like I wasn't moving forward. Of course with me being unemployed after the movie project wrapped up I questioned my situation again and I became extremely sad. I wasn't defeated because I kept sending out my resumes, cover letters and attending networking events. Eventually, I was hired at a hotel as a full time Front Desk Agent and I was extremely excited. I was also hired for a part-time job at the Chicago Urban League as I mentioned to you all before. The full time job was an hour and 30 minutes away from my home but I was still happy. I interviewed for the position at the hotel and I was hired the same day. However, on my first day of the job at the hotel I received a voicemail from the Chicago Urban League stating that the part-time position changed to full-time. Even though the job was still temporary it was a relief to see that the status changed from part-time to full-time. I couldn't stop thanking God and I began to cry because I knew this was a blessing. The Chicago Urban League was only 10-minutes away from my new apartment and the boss who hired me was my previous boss who hired me for a temporary job at The Chicago Urban League, over the summer. I have a great relationship with him and he is the one person I can always count on when it comes to employment. There are several people who always told me they would help me find a job but this man proved it. He proved it by answering my emails, by personally handing my resume to his manager and saying to him,

"If no one believes in this girl I believe in her because she's going to make it. I just feel it in my spirit. She exudes greatness and you need to hire her."

When I found out that my boss said this about me I couldn't stop crying because I knew God was working in my favor again. Mr. Hancock is not only my boss he is the definition of what a mentor and father figure really is. Without hesitation I told my boss at the hotel that I would have to change my status from full-time to part-time but then I thought about the distance I would be traveling, so I decided the best thing for me to do was resign. I resigned from the hotel and two weeks later I went to New York for job training at the Chicago Urban League National Office. The hotel, the flight and food were paid for which was an amazing experience. I know I mentioned this earlier but man I still can't stop thanking God for blessing me with this wonderful job opportunity, because I became a Healthy Living Peer Educator, for the Chicago Urban League. The pay is good and the schedule is flexible too. Working at The Chicago Urban League is definitely a consistent income and it is giving me an opportunity to fund my dream. I was also hired as a part-time Sales Representative at the Field Museum, which I was really excited about too.

After New York and working at the Field Museum I realized that the consistent income I had been praying for was beginning to really become a reality. I was still selling my books, doing my motivational speaking, acting, hosting my talk show and fighting to be an entrepreneur but now I had money to not only pay my bills but to also get me closer to my dreams. Some of my dreams in the next three years are to be financially stable, be married, buy a home and build a flourishing business.

I believe that these goals are obtainable because God has opened doors for me that I thought were nailed shut. He has shown me that I'm closer than I think. That's why I want to reassure you that you're closer than you think.

Your finances may be tough but God has an unlimited supply. Your relationship may be complicated but God will make it simple. You may be single but God is preparing your king or queen, so whenever you feel like you have a problem he already has the solution. You may think that you're far away but you're closer than you think so continue to walk by faith and not by sight. Take control of your life and don't allow any man or woman to direct your path. Be the main character in your movie so you can be known as the creator and not only as creative. Whenever you feel like giving up just pray, journal, speak affirmations and remember you're closer than you think. As a matter of fact, I'll tell you a story about being closer than you think you are to your dreams.

A father, a mother and a daughter traveled the land every year. They visit these beautiful mountaintops and the father decided to get a head start up this mountain. The mountain began to become hard, treacherous and unbearable as the father was climbing up the mountain. The mountain is known for being shaky, extremely rocky, and very slippery. His daughter and wife encouraged him to keep climbing this mountain because neither one of them wanted him to give up on his dream. The father had been trying to reach the top of this mountain for several years because he wanted to prove to himself that greatness does exist within him. The father kept going but then he decided to stop because it became too difficult. He said, "I'll never make it. I'm just going to turn around and go back down." He began to head down the mountaintop but then he heard this still small voice say, "Stop! Wait! Don't give up. You're closer than you think." The father thought about his wife and his daughter and he knew at that moment it wasn't about him anymore. If he gave up not only would he be disappointing himself but he would be crushing the dreams of his family as well. He didn't want his wife and daughter to say if he can't do it then none of us can. He began to get upset and he said to the still small voice "Look, I've been going up this mountain for a while and I haven't reached the top." The still small voice said, "You haven't reached the top but you're closer than you think. If you keep the faith you'll make it. Don't give up on your dreams." The man said, "Ok fine, I'll give it one more try." The man began to go up the mountain again and boy was he struggling.

It was dark, it was freezing cold, it was raining, his knees collapsed and the wind was blowing out of control but he kept hearing a voice say don't give up on your dreams, you're closer than you think. He began to shut his eyes and the very last time he opened up his eyes he was at the top of the mountain. He thought he was going to be alone on that journey but he wasn't because God was there the whole time. He looked back down the mountain and he couldn't see his family but he knew they were there. He fell to his knees and he began to smile. The sun came out, the clouds cleared up and a rainbow came across the sky. He couldn't stop smiling and he began to cry because he finally achieved his dream. For years he had been striving to reach the top of the mountain but he continuously kept making excuses as to why he would never reach the top. He kept thinking that reaching the top of the mountain was about him but it wasn't about him. It was about all the people that would be inspired by his testimony because he never gave up on his dream. He almost gave up but because he believed that he was closer than he thought he was and he realized it wasn't about him he MADE IT!!!! Did it seem impossible? Did it seem unnecessary at times? Did it seem like the odds were against him? Did it seem hard? Did it seem like it wasn't worth it and did it seem like he was never going to finish? Yes to all the questions above but he never allowed his current circumstances to predict his future. He might've been doubtful along the journey like most people are but he never gave up because he knew deep down inside that reaching the top of the mountain would be fulfilling.

Sometimes you have to remind yourself of the tools God has already instilled within you and once you utilize them you will always surpass any obstacle. The father surpassed every obstacle and when he made it back down the mountain his family said, "You did it. We knew you were closer than you thought you were." The father realized that accomplishing his goal empowered him to want to help others to do the same and in life that is what you should seek.

Don't do things for the fame, the money, or a pat on the back but do it because the world needs to see what the definition of service really means. There is a little girl waiting on you to start your mentoring program, there is a little boy searching for a coach so he can learn how to play basketball, there is a sibling who is waiting on you to teach them how to invest their money and there is a parent that is waiting on your book to be published so they can give their child hope that dreams do come true. Acts of service exist everywhere and they begin with you. Ask God how close you are to your dream and when he gives you your answer I guarantee he will have an act of service in his response to you.

Take me for example. I want to be wealthy. I want to be well known like Dr. Martin Luther King. But I don't have to be boastful about it because those things will come if I'm taking action in my community. I don't have to seek recognition because if I'm doing what I need too for others that notoriety will come. I remember when my big brother at the Chicago Urban League told me that and I was shocked. I didn't realize that I was focusing on earning respect, becoming well known and being wealthy so much, that I forgot about the real reason of why I even pursued being a television personality and being involved in the arts.

I never wanted to be a personality or in the arts for the money, the fame or the recognition. If those things came along that was great but the truth is I love interviewing people. I love telling other people's stories and I love making them feel good by sharing their testimony. I love the idea of connecting with someone and finding out we have so much in common. Through my platform of LWOO I want my spirit to be transferred to others so I can help someone else become a speaker, actress, host, entrepreneur or author.

Also, young people we have to be careful with social media because it's a great resource but it can be dangerous. Some people get on social media to network or catch up with old friends but then some people get on social media to entertain gossip or cyber bully another person and that's wrong. The worst part is a lot of the negative energy comes from people idolizing someone else's lifestyle. The reality is we will waste away as humans if we continue to want someone else's path and we don't accept our own. As a role model I have a responsibility to my community. Regardless if I'm receiving a pat on the back or not if that's what I'm passionate about then that's what I need to be doing. I thank God for placing my big brother in my life because he made me realize that it is truly not about me.

I have to give back to God's Kingdom before he blesses me with my happily ever after and that's fine with me because I was put here on this earth to be his faithful servant. Not to judge others or look down on them but to encourage them to be the best version of themselves they can be. My best friend Brittany Jett said, "Her goal in life is to be the best version of herself she can be and if she can accomplish that then she will be happy." And you know what, I agree. I'm closer than I think I am to achieving my dreams but it's because I continue to walk in God's grace and give back to His people everyday by being the best version of me.

Challenge yourself to mentor a young girl, challenge yourself to attend bible study, challenge yourself to eat healthier or exercise and each day share what you do with others because you never know how your journey can inspire someone else. I dare you to be the best version of yourself. If that means fasting from social media, applying for a gym membership, eating healthier foods, stop hanging out on the corner, giving up smoking or reading the bible consistently. Then like Nike says, "Just Do It."

Mark my words you're closer than you think you are to

conquering your dreams so go into over drive to reach the top of that mountaintop. I remember when I was at church one day a pastor said, "Sometimes when the lights go out in life that's an indication that your show is about to start." When he said that one sentence it resonated with my spirit greatly because when that man was going up the mountaintop, it was dark, it was scary and it was very intimidating. But since God spoke directly to him and gave him his assignment, with an act of service attached to it he wasn't going to let darkness take what was designed for him. When something is designed for you no man or woman can take it from you because that goal, that dream, that desire will not fit on him or her. It will either be too big or too small but it will not fit on that person. So when you feel weak and when you are fearful. When you are feeling challenged because you can't see what's in front of you or you can't figure out what's going on, just remember that your show is about to start.

The pastor also said, "God doesn't call the qualified he equips the qualified." The man thought he couldn't make it up the mountaintop and sometimes in life you think you need a famous last name, special powers like a super hero or you say to yourself if I was a millionaire I wouldn't have any problems but sometimes in life it's enough to be YOU.

You don't need the famous last name, the special powers or anything extra from mankind because God has already equipped you with what you need to WIN!!! Ooooohhhh, I'm fired up now. Let me get back on task.

You didn't think you were getting away that easily did you? Grab that pen and paper again!!!

1. Do you feel like you're closer than you think you are to your dream? If so, why?
2. Do you ever feel like giving up? If so, what motivates you to keep going?
3. What's your definition of success? Have you achieved that yet?
4. Do you know how to have a close relationship with your family, friends, teachers, mentees or children?
5. What do you physically, mentally, emotionally, spiritually and nutritionally need to do to get closer to your dreams?

Chapter 4
When Life Happens

When life happens it can be stressful, it can be frustrating and it can be intimidating but as long as you have your foundation established you will never fail. By having your foundation established you will know who you are and what you stand for. Rev. Wells said, "The winds will blow and the storms will come but that house will not fall because it was founded on solid ground. You will be able to build your new life on the foundation of truth. " You won't allow life to stop you because you will begin to understand the trials and tribulations life throws at you. You will build your foundation on truth and you will trust that it won't be broken apart.

I want you to try to put God in the center of your universe because he will always support you. Put God first in everything that you do in life so you can be successful in your future endeavors. When you feel an argument coming on with a co-worker call out to God, when your finances are funny call out to God, when you're having relationship issues call out to God, when you're having trouble forgiving someone call out to God and when you feel like your dreams will never come true call out to God. It's easy to give up but it's hard to keep going. When you call out to God He will give you ongoing ammunition that will never allow you to quit. The fuel He will pour into your soul will never read empty. I would rather have God's approval than to walk around seeking validation from people who don't know half of my story. I would rather have angels in my corner than to have evil spirits interrupting my thought process. If you allow the enemy to interrupt your thought process then you'll be walking around angry because you almost had a vision completed in your mind but you allowed negativity to interrupt it. Does anyone out there have a problem? Well, I would rather have a problem and know that God is working on the solution than to have a problem but no solution because I was afraid to cry out to God. Be fearless and cry out!! Don't remain quiet. Speak up and speak to God. He's waiting to hear from you. Things may not be going right but He is here to help you through this difficult time. He will never leave nor forsake you so have enough courage to tell Him what's on your heart and mind.

So let me ask you these questions. What do you do to deal with life when it happens? Do you work out, do you eat, do you go to sleep, do you go out with friends or do you go on social media? If you do any of these things that's ok but I challenge you to give it to God and pray. Don't allow your stress to over take you because if you do it can cloud your judgment. When life happens it can take you so far off your course that you forget who you are. It's possible for you to accidentally forget your purpose. That's a battle I was constantly dealing with.

For a long time, it was hard for me to accept that God had a different plan for my life. I spent so much time on being a reporter/anchor but I had to trust that God had bigger plans in store for me. Now I'm going full throttle after my speaking career, selling my books, acting, creating a new sound for children by doing motivational rapping, promoting my talk show and being an entrepreneur. As I mentioned earlier, I incorporated my (Not For Profit) LWOO NFP and my (For Profit) which is LWOO Enterprises.

I decided that if life is going to happen I might as well do something that will make me happy and bring me fulfillment. I'm not going to waste time doing anything that is not bringing me joy. Building my brand brings me happiness and giving back to my community brings me fulfillment so it's time for me to figure out how I can do that full time!!! It's time for me to get rid of the excuses because at this point the only person that is holding me back is myself.

Of course you need a main source of income, which is why it's ok to have a job but if that's not what you want to do give yourself a deadline. Personally, I'm done working the jobs that take up too much of my time. If I can put my time, skill set and passion into a job then why can't I put all of that positive energy into creating my own opportunities? Sure it may take a little longer to get the financial gain but it will be worth it because now you can set your own hours, spend time with your family, travel and work hard at doing something you love.

As I stated before when life happens it really pushes you to dig deeper into who you are and it forces you to create opportunities for yourself as well as others. You probably always had thoughts of creating your own real estate business, starting your own record label or owning your own consulting firm. So don't wait until you're laid off to start your business. Don't wait until you are put out to start thinking about buying your first home. A sorority sister of mine said,

"Plan for the worst and hope for the best means just that; planning ahead so that if the devil comes in trying to shake your ground you have a strong foundation and can move along as if nothing ever happened."

When life happens take that negative experience or that negative person and use that as ammunition to create a great legacy that can't be torn down. My motto is: To impact lives, change communities and leave behind a POWERFUL legacy. I'm on a mission to empower youth to become entrepreneurs. What's yours? I believe we deserve to be financially free from debt, student loans and bills. We shouldn't be stressed about finances, education, living expenses and traveling. If you put in work to have all of that and more then you deserve to receive RESULTS!!!!

As a matter of fact, remember how I told you guys about how I chased an agent and finally got signed? I forgot to tell you that five months after being signed I was let go. I was told that I was let go because the agency needed to down size their roster and they were also having trouble marketing me because I'm multi-faceted. I was devastated and truly heart broken but then a month later I realized they did me a favor.

With them letting me go it just added another bullet point to my resume of how I could overcome another obstacle. I took that disappointment, those insecurities, that feeling of hopelessness and started searching for new talent agencies to apply to. If you are involved in the arts you know that it is hard to get an agent but after I sent my stuff out I heard back from three of the five agencies I applied to. I sent out my resume, my cover letter, my book and my headshot. I knew I had to spice up my audition materials by including my book in the submission package and it earned me a response from three agencies. I auditioned for two of them and by the grace of God I was signed with a new talent agency on Feb. 17, 2016. Two in a half hours after I left the audition they emailed me and said, "Congratulations we want to welcome you to our talent agency as an on camera talent." I said, "Wow look at God." Every time I receive a no and I don't accept it he always rewards me by showing me who is in charge of my destiny. He has arranged the steps I need to take in life and sometimes there may be some failures but He will always pull a success card out of his hat like a magician to prove that you are on the right track.

On April. 13, 2016 I was accepted into Black Box Academy, which is the most prestigious acting training program in Chicago. Once again I couldn't stop thanking God. February was a great month for me but also in February I had an allergic reaction to my eye. I'm allergic to peanuts and I was rubbing my eye so much that I popped a blood vessel. My eye was completely red and I was extremely self-conscious about it. I felt like everyone was stirring at me and it made me feel uncomfortable. I was constantly wearing sunglasses because I didn't want anyone to see my eye.

I had a photo-shoot coming up in March that my talent agency booked for me and I had an audition for the Black Box Academy. I just knew my eye wasn't going to be healed for the photo-shoot or the audition but God never fails. Do you know my eye was healed by the time I had my photo-shoot and my audition? Here I was panicking and not confident because the two eye doctors that I saw kept saying it was going to take months for it to heal but God had already ordered my steps. He knew what the outcome would be and he answered my prayers.

Don't allow life or in my case a freak accident to change the steps God has already ordered for you. When you hear that evil spirit in your ear making you envious of others, unforgiving, self-conscious and always thinking negative thoughts do something that the devil isn't expecting. Give someone a compliment, forgive an enemy, listen to some uplifting music, love on yourself a little more, send an unexpected gift to someone's doorstep and share your knowledge or wealth with others. When life happens you don't allow it to defeat you but instead you defeat it.

Through spirituality we must worship him.

Through health we must take care of our bodies so we can be around for our children and their children's children.

Through our mentalities we must feed knowledge to our brains so that we can have a mindset that won't perish.

Through our physicality's we must build endurance so that we can understand how to overcome pain by remaining in the fight and through our emotions we must build discernment so that we know how to control our behaviors.

These five pillars can really change your life and if we focus on them more they will become apart of our everyday routine. It's not easy but it's better to start practicing these qualities now than to procrastinate for 10 or 20 years about what changes you should have made. So grab that journal again and let's keep writing.

1. As a kid what vision did you have for your life?
2. Has your vision turned out the way you expected? If not, then what are you going to do to fix it?
3. When life happened, how did you take control of it instead of life taking control of you?
4. Why do you care about what other people think? Or do you not care at all?
5. Even though it hurts to experience losses, disappointment and failures, how does it feel to know that you survived?

Chapter 5
Accepting Where I Am

Wow, how can I begin this chapter? Talk about one of the hardest things to do in LIFE!!!! It was extremely hard for me to accept where I am because I couldn't believe that becoming a reporter/anchor wasn't my calling. Never in a million years did I ever think I would be doing a 180 to pursue being an entrepreneur. I knew that was going to be my future plans but I always thought that journalism would be the route I would take to get there. Boy, did that backfire. I was scared, angry and confused all at the same time. I couldn't understand how my plan didn't work out because I thought I chose the more practical route, which was journalism instead of acting. As a result, I spent a lot of time fighting to become a reporter/anchor when God was taking me down a different path. God really wanted me to replant that seed and grow it into something bigger and better. He wanted me to go back to speaking, writing, hosting, acting, rapping, singing, dancing and inspiring others to step into their greatness.

God already knew what my struggle was going to be He just needed me to accept it. Even though I didn't want to He forced me to do it anyway. I doubted His plan for my life and I ran away from it, He wouldn't allow me to get a reporter/anchor job. It wasn't until 2014 I finally decided to listen to him. Once I stepped out on faith everything fell into place. He blessed me with paid speaking engagements, He allowed me to meet the right people who gave me the platform to build teen writing workshops, He made sure I did my first music video, He got my talk show off the ground, He gave me the idea of my inspirational posts, He built my website, He gave me a management team, He blessed me to get signed with a talent agency, He pushed me to start my non profit-for profit, He gave me a job at the Chicago Urban League, He even made it possible for me to move into my first apartment, and He gave me the will power to write a second book. God has taken me to the next level and it's because I trusted in his word. Sure I have had my moments where I've doubted his plan, doubted my finances and doubted if I was good enough to receive his praise but I AM worthy to be praised!!

I'm worthy of his praises and so are you. Whatever it is that you doubt in your life don't doubt it anymore. Plan to succeed, live to achieve, and execute your task flawlessly. Don't think about what will happen if you fail just focus on the possibilities of succeeding. Start writing your acceptance speech for when you get your first award at the Grammys or even the Oscars. Even though it may seem like it is impossible for a minority to win an Oscars you can start writing your acceptance speech now because it still can be YOU. Start looking for your new outfit that you're going to where on The Steve Harvey Show, start selling tickets for people to come to your next event and start writing thank you cards to people for supporting you because in your mind you have ALREADY MADE IT!!!! Once you accept where you are there is no human that can destroy your state of mind. Once you accept where you are YOU become the most powerful being alive because you understand God's purpose for your life. You may be in a season of relationship trouble, friendship issues, financial stress or work trauma but you'll be happy in the midst of it because you know the season is temporary. The only reason why the season may seem to last forever is because you haven't accepted where you are but once you do God will say YOU PASSED THAT TEST MY CHILD and move you on to the next task. See, life is all about lessons and God needs you to learn from that lesson so that you can teach someone else how to overcome it.

I'm a firm believer that everything happens for a reason and God will never give you more than what you can handle. Some things happen for a reason, a season and a lifetime and you just have to wait for God to reveal which season you're in. God will continue to feed you as long as you continue to feed yourself and others. You won't run on empty because your soul will be filled with his loving energy and overflowing spirit. Haven't you ever wondered how someone who is homeless, who has lost a parent, been diagnosed with a disease or experienced violence can keep smiling and be a blessing to someone else? It's because they know THE LORD!!!! They have accepted where they are and they will not allow anyone or anything to stand in their way because they're on a mission to influence the world. Accepting where you are can be difficult but once you do you will be one step closer to achieving God's goal for your life.

I'm almost done with the questions guys just hang in there. NO, I'm not. Sooooooo, grab that journal again or maybe you should just keep it close by. Here are the questions.

1. Have you accepted where you are? If not, why?
2. How does it feel to be in this chapter of your life?
3. Are you ready to move forward or are you content with where you are?
4. Do you think this level is all God has for you?
5. What are you looking forward to as far as your dreams, goals and visions?

Chapter 6
Giving Yourself Credit

I can't believe we made it to the last chapter already but I can't say this enough GIVE YOURSELF CREDIT!!!!! I know it's difficult because I'm the queen of being hard on myself but I have learned that if I don't give myself credit for what I've already done I will never appreciate the blessings that God is going to give me!! God needs you to appreciate what he is already doing for you and what he is about to do for you. He needs to know that you trust him, even when things are tough. It's easy to blame yourself when things aren't panning out the way you want them to and sometimes it's even easier to blame others, but you shouldn't. When you feel yourself about to sink into a hole call out to God for help and he will erase any feeling of envy, hate, frustration, anger or doubt.

You will begin to recognize that things could've been worse and you're lucky to just be breathing. Can you imagine not being able to breathe? I know we have all had a moment when we have jumped in a pool and when you were swimming back up it took you longer than you expected to reach the surface. For a second you might've thought I'm going to drown, I'm not going to make it and why is this taking so long? But none of that mattered because you just kept swimming until you could reach the top, right? Why treat life any differently? You're alive so you have the ability to keep fighting for your dream everyday! You have a support system and you woke up this morning, so you're blessed! You have the chance to inspire one more person and the opportunity to teach someone something. You get the opportunity to fix a mistake and make it right again, so give yourself credit for graduating college, give yourself credit for writing that book, give yourself credit for working two jobs, give yourself credit for being a great single mom and give yourself credit for being able to stay true to who you are.

Sometimes we overlook our talent because we say to ourselves anyone can do this but the reality is everyone can't. Everyone doesn't have the ability to be a pastor, a teacher, a lawyer, a doctor or a musician. It takes a special person to do every job and once you figure out your calling you will begin to give yourself credit because you know in your heart that you do it well. When you figure out what your talent is you won't be able to compare yourself to others because God gave all of us different ingredients to make sure we are all unique.

For example, when a movie is being produced you need

a writer, actors, a director, a sound crew and much more. All of these people bring something different to the table and that's what makes a great movie. When you work together and understand everyone's talent you can all become one. There is no reason to compete, be envious, judge others or put someone down because together we can all make a difference. Utilize your skillset, work with others and give yourself credit for understanding what it means to be different but also for sharing yourself with others. Give yourself credit for instilling wisdom into others, for empowering others, for starting a business that could give more people jobs and for being the change in your community that you always wanted to see. You are the creation that we've been waiting for so please don't give up on your dreams because the world is waiting for your invention, your style, your voice and your mindset. You may not see it but God sees your vision and how you can get closer to achieving that vision is by giving yourself credit every step of the way.

We made it to the last chapter AAAAAAHHHHHH here are the last set of questions.

1. Do you give yourself credit? If not, why?
2. Are you extremely hard on yourself? If so, why?
3. Do you ever take time to realize how amazing you truly are?

4. Do you love the talents and gifts God gave you? Do you know what they are?
5. Do you give others credit and do you expect it in return when you've done well?

Snaps fingers. I feel like we just aired out a lot guys and I'm so proud of all of you. I hope one day I can meet all of you but thank you so much for supporting me along my journey by reading my books. Look out for my next book ladies and gentleman because from now on, I will be teaching you how to write a book, how to host a teen writing workshop, how to create a business plan, how to become a motivational speaker and how to run a successful business. Stay tuned you guys because as I continuously work my way to the top I'm taking YOU with me!! I leave you with this:

"Live, laugh and shake it off. Just LWOO on it."

By: LWOO (Learning Wisdom Optimism & Opportunity).

About the Publisher

Let us bring your story to life! With Life to Legacy, we offer the following publishing services: manuscript development, editing, transcription services, ghostwriting, cover design, copyright services, ISBN assignment, worldwide distribution, and eBooks.

Throughout the entire production process, you maintain control over your project. We are here to serve you. Even if you do not have a manuscript, we can ghostwrite your story for you from audio recordings or legible handwritten documents.

We also specialize in family history books, so you can leave a written legacy for your children, grandchildren, and others. You put your story in our hands, and we'll bring it to literary life! We have several publishing packages to meet all your publishing needs. Call us at: 877-267-7477, or you can also send e-mail to: Life2Legacybooks@att.net. Please visit our Web site: www.Life2Legacy.com

www.ingramcontent.com/pod-product-compliance
Lightning Source LLC
Chambersburg PA
CBHW051714040426
42446CB00008B/888